I0170236

Songs of a Clerk

Gary Beck

Winter Goose
Publishing

Winter Goose Publishing
2701 Del Paso Road, 130-92
Sacramento, CA 95835

www.wintergoosepublishing.com
Contact Information: info@wintergoosepublishing.com

Songs of a Clerk

COPYRIGHT © 2014 by Gary Beck

First Edition, June 2014

Cover Art by Winter Goose Publishing
Typeset by Odyssey Books

ISBN: 978-1-941058-16-9

Published in the United States of America

To A.L.B.

Boredom a disease
Action a cure
Don't ail

Table of Contents

Greeley Square

Tiny islet in a maddened swirl,
lunch tide refugees
clot your drab benches.
The buses, cars, trucks
passioning the city
honk slumbering ears awake,
cloud your triangle of sootness
painting funerals of sad sitters.
The office exiles,
grey-suited and bitter,
have sagging mouths,
soiled tan raincoats.
They sit on pigeon dung
faces turned to the receding sun
and when the sun turns coy,
putting a translucent hand of cloud
before his face,
stare the packaged shoppers
and young girls from out-of-town.
This nibble of safety
stolen from the city,
a fractional oasis,
a grassless park.

Casualty

This evening she will come,
the dark-haired girl I adore.
She promised.
I sit a Baron of power
dreaming her perfect,
but the drabness of my office day
smashes my vision
and leaves me at my desk,
a victim of my pencils.

Bewildered

The eternal clerk of boredom,
master of his desk,
shuffles slowly through his papers,
thinking of sunny beaches.
He will never know
empires,
passions,
contentment,
just the same daily march
to office, to lunch,
to home, to sleep,
suspicioning the theft of joy.

Pavan

Sitting at my desk, my eyes begin to close,
I doze a fantasy.
The music makes me forest groves.
Two hundred years ago
the wild gypsy whirled
in swot, salacious dance.

Carried by a jaded serpent
so fast I overtake my soul,
I build bigger heavens for monks.

Undeath ready
I curse, I cry,
with ineluctable magic power
cull the gods,
who reborn me.

The straw hat
of too much shade
never lets the little prince grow up.

The dream of three men in a tub
who talk Oedipus.
Two had mothers,
one was prissy,
sipping tea in a tempest of libido.

Armless, legless swirl of gypsy,
sphere of torporous rotation,
your earth supine,
your death forever falling.

The men who watch
lust your limbless body.

Sunlight opens my pyrotic eyes.
Saboteurs creep by
armed with bombs and axes.
I am frightened and return to work.

Clerk's Plea

Should I fall upon my sharpened pencil,
No. 2 lead?
Should I leap upon my desk and scream?
Terrify everyone
until they yell: "You're fired!"
Help me.
What shall I do to escape
the tedious, soul sucking
office.

Drifting

I hear them all day long,
the office workers trapped and lonely,
bantering their silly jokes,
babbling to devour the day,
weakening in bored moments
and boasting of past feats
and glorified ambitions.
They go home in the evening
blighted by papers
and unfulfillment.
Pondering elusive pasts
once of pride and power,
heat a frozen dinner,
hide before the TV set,
finally a sigh,
the preview of tomorrow,
turn off the light
and lose themselves
in sleep.

Journey

Whither goest, wanderer?
So rarely asked
when head down,
shoulders hunched, back bent,
knees bowed, feet flat,
shuffling,
from bed
to job,
play,
sex,
sin,
sleep,
disturbing little.

Testimonial

Carbon-copy clerk
of haunted hours
and surreptitious fantasies,
you of nine-to-five soul,
can't be late,
millions in a Swiss vault,
waiting till the FBI forgets.
Sore feet . . .
Backache . . .
Flatulence . . .
I have seen you countless times,
on lunchtime avenues and streets
in foreign lands and my land,
grey, bewildered, empty,
awaiting instructions.

The Boss

Sixty stories high
my power overlooks the city.
For my amusement
parades prance below.
How drab the soldiers pass.
The scarlet band
of high steps and stuttering drums
flaunts yellow banners,
but I watch, a bored giant,
finding no smalltown, homespun,
native American thrill.

Relic

When she walks
a funny little whisk,
somewhere twixt the waist and hips
tells that once ago
men looked damp beds at her.
Now on tiny cut-glass toes
she tinkles through the office,
daft and nice.
She so admired Queen Victoria
and never heard of molecules,
but so what.
She would still drop clouds of dust,
an antique going to be passioned.

Leave of Absence

Irrepressible derelict
humming to himself
on the brief ferry ride,
as business-suit commuters
stare envious, resentful
at drunken irresponsibility,
cheerful rejection
of nine-to-five bondage
and home-to-suburban prison.
Demeaning the ride of serious travelers,
he grins in derision
at blank office faces,
then rolls an empty beer can
down the aisle of escape.

Plaint

Often in the boredom of my office
I think about the ancient Chinese poets,
remote, delicate, and serene.
As I wait,
impatient to make my poems,
I see parchment men of long-lost graces
sipping wine, in discourse,
reaching for pen and ink,
making incredible songs.
I do not yearn for T'ang.
Li Po, Po Chu I, Tu Fu
are sleeping sentiments to never come again,
but sometimes I cry for the beauty
absent from this life.

City Speck

Old man of Greely Square
trapped in dirt and madness,
you raved strange words
of green leaves with many eyes,
and of what profit is a man and woman.
You stopped before me
staring me through drunken fumes,
drooling mouth accusing me,
twitching hands begging pity,
until I fled to office shame.
All afternoon I heard the well-fed voices,
the bright dresses
stuffed with breasts and thighs,
the dark suits
of hairless legs and paunches,
and thought of you all day,
until near home
the sound of children's laughter
quite erased you.

The Clerk's Song

Hidden in the only ally, unbiased sleep,
the sudden summons rips my exile's cave.
The clock that serves employers cries:
Arise! Dazed, apologetic, I mumble:
"Five minutes." Silence the insistent nag,
my wife of passing ticks.
Stir awake. Oh, no. Overslept.
Fast wash, dry shave, yesterday's suit,
breakfastless rush to the bus,
the guilty fears of lateness.
"Will he see me sneaking in?
"Will he fire me?"
Off the bus,
following the tardy hips of typists
to the subway of suffering.
The brief pause in daylight,
the radiant sungleams unnoticed,
scurry through revolving doors,
"Good morning," to the elevator man,
archbishop of boredom.
My floor, entrance, trying to look
as if I just stepped out for coffee.
The potent eye of accusation falls on me
and I take refuge at my desk.
Sightless, I stare at my papers
(my face my mask of concentration)
dreaming time's faster passage,
yet fearful of its passing.

Greeley Square II

Greeley Square at lunchtime,
dreary and severe,
the office workers
drabber than pigeons,
the out-of-towners
lost in their clothing.
The black men
wearing radios, caps, and sneakers,
pushing handcarts and resentment.
The Spanish men
read jokebooks in the doorways.
The old men sit upon the benches,
pale and flimsy in the sun
and gather newspapers and empty bags,
after the clerks return to work.

Office Procedure

Bent over our desks
racing to our doom
the work piles high.
Peeking through the fog
the boss smiles down,
sadistic as God
peeking at Adam.
"Good morning, sir . . . Hem, hem.
"We're real busy this morning.
"Think we'll get some help?
"Oh, no. We can handle it . . .
"I just meant . . .
"We will, sir."
Obsequious betrayer,
feeble enemy,
my tongue.

Escape

Voices shrill and laughing,
blare of happy music
people walk the stairs.
I, on bed of visions,
more opiumed than parchment sages
build of my fancies a power.
My eyes grown heavy, blink.
My body sags toward sleep,
a poor clerk's kingly peace.
Gone the waste of office prison,
useless yearning for a woman,
desolation from a wordless night.
The restless torment slumbers.
Triumphs are woven from afar,
lured by drowsy device.
I am old men in the sun,
brown, crinkled, juiceless,
thoughting nothing.

Yearning

Last night,
close to a woman of softness,
my sad power of dreaming rested,
her hunger my peace.
Today,
trapped in office prison,
I listen to foolish prattle
and fear she will not come again.

Égalité

The strange after-work daze
in the flood haste of city men,
answering the hearth call of evening
to the wife of love,
the children of consolation.
Does anyone return to this?
I am adrift
on this alien subway,
alone, rocking, dozing.
Do the rocking, dozing people
at whom I stare
and who stare at me
feel the same?
Is this dreamer of empires
everyone?

Illusion

Looking from a window
on the sixtieth floor,
I see the strange city,
make-believe and gritty.
I am a feudal lord
scanning his power,
bound by rivers
and a baby lake.
Traffic is moving.
If I stretch one giant hand,
I can move anything below.

Departure

My last day,
farewell, farewell,
machine of endless appetite,
eater of my soul,
indifferent as any corporation
that devoured my day,
farewell.

Pledge

Metal lover that I tend,
mistress of my nine-to-five soul,
when I cheat you of your due,
do you notice?
Are you lonely in your sterile brain
when I, unwilling servant,
shun your tape of meaningless transmission?
Does some omnipotent machine record my sin?
Careless overseer, outsmarted by a serf.
Brief stolen moments until I go home,
where I'll plan all night
to visit you with bombs and axes.

Terminal Leave

I sit quietly at my desk,
do they think I'm working?
A mad bomber,
poems in pocket
lusting to explode.
The coffee bell rings twice,
salivate, salivate.
While the long line forms,
I slip an incandescent poem
into the coffee urn of atonement
and watch my co-workers burn their mouths,
drop their cups,
melt away.

Revenge

I am the eternal clerk
posting his doomsday figures,
the last figment
of dreary imagining.
Hidden by my carbon face,
a lurking dream
steals the morning minutes
of my employer's time.

Oppression

I sit in unemployment office,
forced to patience, and brought low.
The old man of no joy
knows his power and makes me wait.
He has never known
sunsets, white beaches,
a girl's laughter in the moonlight,
the smiles of children,
just tyranny over the jobless.

Treadmill

Home the huskless workers go,
buried in the evening journals,
sitting row on row in subways.
Only the iron wheel's cry
enters their silent shell,
grey, drained, soporific,
fancying the peace of home,
but knowing with a piteous dread
tomorrow comes today again.

Escape II

How can I endure this waste
when I am daily trapped
from nine to five?
What is more futile than a clerk
dreaming of Pericles?
There, I said it, Pericles.
I will scream snow-capped mountains,
perched on a mammoth,
seeking mysteries.
Yet I sit
in one of the world's wonders,
The Empire State Building,
(though it's diminishing)
dreary, altogether drab,
waiting for release
at quitting time.

Anticipation

Toil dreamer, toil.
Today machines run
hot and fast,
served by aging fingers.
Tired old Dave,
consumptive,
shows yellow-specked photographs:
"I wanted to be someone,
"have my own house in The Bronx.
"But look at me now,
"weak heart, ailing wife,
"soon too old.
"The machine needs nimble fingers.
"What will I do then?
"Where are the things
"I used to dream about?
"Soon I lay me down to sleep,
"no memories to keep me company,
"in an eternity of idleness."

Service

Clickety clack,
clickety clack
move the robot fingers,
teletype of monsters
spouting as some oracle of old,
fat-bellied and perverse.
Clickety clack,
the message is coming,
rush to obey it.
Scuttle servants,
in a clerk's drab genuflection.
Hours to go,
the clock moves slow.
The boss is watching.
Faster, faster,
clickety clack,
an agony of words,
dull and coded commerce.
Nothing of adventure.
"No desperate spy
"trapped in talons of intrigue."
Clickety clack.
Ship one, purchase two.
Clickety clack.
Time to go.
Goodnight Jim, Tony, Dave . . .
Clickety cla . . .

Decline

Our crippled sons
do not have their forefathers' crusades.
They whine the ancient songs,
wheezing in their heated rooms.
They cry for causes,
but curse the test-tube plans
that guide us to new motions.
They would be led,
spearmen in Agamemnon's band,
these tiring office mites,
who would sack a city.
Fanciers of fair captives,
yearning for distant glory,
not even the poet's song
can make epic of their dullness.

Summons

We sit in the park,
the tired, dreary clerks
at lunchtime,
briefly dreaming in the sun.
We watch the senseless
wandering of pigeons,
the young girls,
our juiceless neighbors.
The nearest clock
chimes a summons.
Time to go.
We fold our newspapers
and return to work.

Sentenced

The dreary clerk
returned again to office prison,
the mindless waste of nine-to-five,
the endless fellow worker drivel,
the brief reprieve at lunchtime,
too soon done.
How to sing of green fields,
tall Pacific mountains,
birthing a mighty ocean,
when no one listens
to pleas for parole.

Greeley Square III

I sit in Greeley Square,
exile of my lunchtime.
I stare at the shoppers
and the office workers,
pasty in the pale spring sun.
The honking, roaring traffic
woos the littered streets.
The shower of soot
bathing the city
in tiny grey-black particles
falls on park sitters,
benched and silent,
watching the clock
until lunch hour is done.

Captured

Again desire gallops hostile Indians 'round me.
My fingers dream safaris.
But the dark overseer lifts his whip
and I sullenly return to work.

Condemned

Man of my rheumatic days,
who sits at office desk
adoze, adrift
on some lost continent,
flooded by machine seepage.
The distant voices of creaky clerks,
shrill and chatty girls,
the torpor until five o'clock.
Then out into that lost day's air,
the quick awakening from canned breathing
and I am released,
until imprisonment tomorrow.

Vengeance

On this dreary afternoon,
in the desert of imagination,
I summon Gengis Khan
and Tartar host.
See my power.
I command them.
Slaughter the boss,
the babbling secretaries,
cut out their tongues,
rape and pillage.
Don't let that one escape,
the office idiot.
Some dire torture must be his.
Let him be crucified
by his protruding ears,
for awful jokes.

Retirement

Fat lady of corporate thighs,
rolling your amicable mouth
at passing mailboys.
I watch your unplucked fruit
lurk at loamless desks,
finally shriveling,
as puckered and pursey
as unkissed mouths.
You depart after thirty years,
wristwatch in one hand,
geiger counter in the other.

Disaster

The people in my office
laugh and chatter all day long.
They are not typewriters,
adding machines, duplicators.
Just bodies, salesmen,
clerks, secretaries,
intent on business,
while I puissant navigator
founder on an iceberg.

Distraction

The office smells of old age,
resentful men and women,
chokes the air,
burning my throat,
tearing my eyes,
until I cannot see
my desk of responsibility.

Crash Landing

The clerk of no wings,
sitting at a dreary office desk,
dozing over papers,
sometimes preening
for the secretarial flock,
will suddenly spread great plumes
soaring way aloft,
prince of cloudless visions,
until the boss's voice
ends his flight.

Struggle

Migratory,
job to job,
room to room,
un-Midas fingers
breaking on stale sandwiches.
The clerk of famished roots,
victim of implacable foes,
unreasonable desires.

Pettiness

This fruitless job, planned
by some angel of despair,
bursting his halo with joy at my anguish.
Secure in his triumph,
he gloats on his cloud,
but then I spite him
and quit without notice.

Risk

The grey song of the morning subway,
"stand impaled upon your neighbor's horns,"
the implacable charge to work,
then the ambush is sprung
on defenseless dreamers,
an endangered species.

Time

The creeping, sullen fingers
of my unloving clock
point my life away,
falling with a sad droop
on seven a.m.
(stumble awake, shuffle to work)
then noon, quick lunch,
the drowsy, mindless waiting until five,
then home to watch your uncaring hands
tick away tomorrows.

Continuation

Another job,
sameness of subway.
Will the people of journeys
continue to see me?
The old woman of umbrella legs
thinks I should be in a car by myself.
I sing the last serenade
at my station of surrender.

Temp

Temporary gypsy
alone in unknown office,
they talk distant people past me.
Armed with sharpened pencils
and dreary figures,
I sit a mindless computer,
leering at five o'clock.

Hold Out

The city wanderer
courses the subway crush,
the shoppers flow,
with a nine-to-five soul.
Body trapped by office walls,
awaits with secret hope
the moment of breakout.

Defeat

The clerk of dreary days
eats his two-dollar lunch
ringed by grey faces, tan raincoats.
His freedom hour quickly passes.
It rains. He has nowhere to go.
Lingering over coffee poisons dreams.
The sad faces frighten him.
He rushes outside,
woos the bored streets,
searching the scurrying faces,
staring the sidewalks.
A beautiful woman looks at him.
He stares her full of alpine jaunts.
She only sees his hunger,
looks away.
lost again,
he returns to work.

Greeley Square IV

The dreariest of clerks
goes to lunch in a twenty dollar suit,
then sits in the sun in Greeley Square.
The shabby people line the benches,
victims of the city pigeons.
Weary and depressed,
he tries in vain to lose his office,
but fellow-workers find his refuge
and smash the hope of escape.
Finally they leave.
Ten minutes left to dream.
An elegant woman slowly passes,
vacations in her handbag.
He stares foreign lands and jewels at her.
She doesn't see him.
More than defeated,
he returns to work.

The Office

Sameness of day
in the clerk's crypt,
windowless . . . stale . . . grey . . .
The door opens . . . More work.
Closes . . . Less Joy.

Tompkins Square Park

The summer streets of playing children
mock my tired, after-work body
slumping home, bed-bound, unpark caring.
The refuse on my building's steps
extorts remembrance of trees and grass.
Cheating weariness, I woo stone benches.
In the park, the breastless mothers wear sandals;
their blond children never saw a washcloth.
The Spanish boys gracefully play baseball,
yelled at by crazed old women,
whose children have fled to the Bronx.
The old Italian men wait for death in the sun.
They talk and belch and think of death's black horses,
while their strong children conquer the city.
The people coming home from work . . . A young girl,
thighs outlined in a pink and white striped dress.
The housewives going home to hate their ovens.
Little boys tormenting a wino,
mocking his shopping cart of Muscatel bottles.
Young girls, bare-armed and bare-legged,
thinking of their boyfriends' hands.
Everyone intent on someone . . .
The red-flame sun of boredom sinks
to rest on purple cushions
and I go home, alone.

Illusion II

Fog cuts off my view.
From the sixtieth floor window,
the high altitude swirls
conceal a captive city.
Peering desperately
I fear the world has disappeared,
leaving me at my darkening desk,
an aging baron,
exiled from my land below.

Endurance

O dreamers lost,
adrift in twentieth century madness,
living the myth of city days,
but seeking forgotten truths.
Timeless hungers found in books,
often betray our duller selves.
Exiled nine to five,
weak in loss prevention,
five stolen days each week,
we wake at morning
fearing joblessness and failure,
dreary refugees, grey and crazed,
awaiting the weekend.

Retirement II

Dave leaves today.
Tired Dave.
Machine of strange hunger,
sucking the last juices
from a weary old man.
He makes bad jokes:
"This priest you see,
"he had a good-lookin' blonde
"in the choir . . ."
Old Dave,
home to unkind hearth,
hating his wife, idleness,
the mystery that stole his youth.

Retirement III

Dave's gone.
Unmissed,
vague as memory grows.
Machines clack on,
new fingers serve them,
tireless, devoted.
Yes, the old man's gone.
No sunlight gleams in prison room.
Grey men of inky fingers,
where are your carbons?
The stale, airless room,
unchanging chores,
tired five p.m. expectation,
lucky Dave.

Tempt Me Not

Daylight seen in the distance
through office windows
filtering hope.
Clacking through the thin wood door
machine reminders of obligation:
work, earn money, dress well,
use more credit cards.
Oh, dreary tempter
who no longer offers flesh or glory,
you are paunched, Satan,
from sitting behind your new computer.

Breakdown

Machines of tireless affliction,
you have stopped working.
Your clacking has ended.
We wait, we wait,
as consecrate as priests
in silent aftermath of mass.
Evasive eyes, insect nervous,
no work, nothing to do.
Time clock of each minute clicking,
restless (even fill-in is done),
bored (nothing pleases on debted time),
apprehensive (put book away if the boss comes in).
The thwarted clack of machines unworking.
The passage of time . . . slow . . .
Punctuated each minute by clicks,
waiting for the hand to reach five p.m.
We are barely sentient,
suspended in our garden.

Destiny

I sit impatient as a panther
naked in a tiny cage,
trapped for public entertainment,
pacing, restless for escape.
I pride myself too much,
I am no fierce, feared monarch,
watched with honored fascination.
I have never been that lithe conceit.
Not I, the drab clerk of office days,
the rootless poet of lost nights,
the poor failure of proud endeavors,
prince of squalor,
not yet lost to hope.

Homeward Bound

So days done.
Rush to crosstown shuttle,
eight horses, twenty men,
then to west side express,
of no romantic journeys,
elbow the legless man on roller skates,
a seat . . . quick . . . beat ya, lady.
Whew. Do my feet ache.
Don't meet the eyes of standing women,
indignant as virgin martyrs,
then scan fellow travelers.
The old man in baggy trousers,
alpine hat and paper bundles;
sophisticated lady,
hair by Frank Lloyd Wright;
typists chewing gum;
two insolent young hoods;
lower case executives,
chained to shiny black attaché cases;
the thinker, sneakily peering
from east of his eyelids.
Are we appreciating him?
Rock across the bridge,
as fragile as our days.
The last Manhattan lights
ominous, magical, leading
to the rude serpent mouth
of gaping Brooklyn.
Maiden of the dark eyes

and slender legs,
at whom I stare
and who stares at me,
if I speak,
your little red mouth,
candied and erotic,
will bray some strange dialect,
leaving me more remote
than any outcast.
So I sit,
head nodding in kindred doze
with city pilgrims huddling close,
drowsing thoughtless, drained.
I awaken. No. Three more stops.
So many staring sightlessly,
or cowering behind books and papers.
Last wistful look, farewell dark-eyed maiden,
gone forever in our millioned hive,
farewell.

Change

Undelirious change of jobs,
the same shuffle of dull papers.
Sixty stories high I sit
and envy the birds
circling Central Park.
The stolen moment staring,
then the drone voice,
the overseer of dreary clerks,
compels my return
to files of entombment.

Revery

Sitting in the cafeteria,
brief parole from prison office,
remembering the Pacific Ocean . . .
Days on cold beaches, sea-lion full.
San Francisco, Montara, Half Moon Bay . . .
All have changed, including Monterey.
When I sat at cliff's edge,
ocean near, and heard the wave crush
and smelled the foam rush
and trembled the night away
in fear and rapture
that could not capture
my image of tomorrows,
then I awakened
and trudged back to work.

Ready For . . .

O clockface, I wish I dared
to amputate your hands.
Strangle your vocal corded
seven a.m. scream:
up, up brief sleeper,
the hillside's dew pearled.
No heat again, so in my blue
undainty feet, shower,
watch them turn pink;
draw first blood with toothbrush,
second with razor.
Get dressed.
Yesterday's shirt and jacket,
no one will notice the frayed elbow.
Now go . . .
Forgot to dine, my prince,
snapping, crackling, popping breakfast,
then off . . .
First cigarette, headachy, bitter.
Ready for the subway charge,
hooves set, horns lowered, dash . . .
"Oh. Excuse me, ma'am"
(next time, move).
Times Square shuttle.
I walk the last mile.
I come, elevator of ascension,
and my heart's labor.
The computers click welcome.
I am ready for robotry . . .
Program me . . .

Break

Crouched upon my desk of morning
cake my arms unwilling did receive,
the coffee hour of doom.
They drift like schools of jellyfish,
the violet slithers of light
fluttering tentacles through the waves,
as they approach nutrition.
Insensate stretched across my cup,
my largest toe speaks parables,
completely ignored
in the tidal movement.

Brief Flight

O tiny hat
perched upon a tiny
subway head,
while you read your book,
the bird of kindness
flutters . . . gasps . . .
and falls on emaciated avenues.
The sharp beak
passes through the concrete,
pierces our unyielding streets,
plunges through the subway car
landing at my feet
with a dying thud.
I pick you up and cry:
"Messenger. Frail prophet.
"For the last flight
"there are not wings enough."

Isolation

Doomed to tall buildings,
we perch high in glass towers
and never look down
at the squalor below.

Memory

All day, captive, unwanted,
I sat at prison desk.
Your smell rose from me
love-tired, yet tingling.
No one else but me
smelled perspiring forests.
I held you tightly,
a frail bird of memory,
who dropped feathers on my hand.

Retainer

An elderly lady employee
slowly passes the water cooler
in an old black shroud,
diligently incongruous
in this modern office
of illicit coffee breaks.

Trapped

The sad clerk sings
of antiseptic employment,
trapped by filing cabinets.
Hope dwindles to adding machines,
as surrounding office walls conspire
to smash the dream of flight.

Springtime

The old women of the office
talk coffee and cigarettes
(on ten minute break
how much to say),
but their urgent tongues fall silent
when I shout: "It's spring.
"Let's sing, or swill wine,
"or put on new sneakers
"and run with children."
But they don't listen.
Ladies, already being nudged
by impatient worms,
shut your mouths and listen:
"It's spring."

Ineffectual Flight

Without provision
for your wanton evolution
I escape in fantasy.
I joined the ragged column
marching to Caucasian mines
leaving an effete posterity
to console you.
I cower from the lash
of brutal overseers
until I learn
that this vacation must end.
I send my thoughts
to the Côte d'Azur,
day sun-streaked to the crotch,
night bodice groping to the moon,
grasp prominent parts,
join them in one copulative thrust
and wake up shattered,
back at my desk.

Dulled

Dreary lassitude,
the great ailment, indulgence,
wraps an unconcerned serpent around me.
I hover through my office day
sick and bored,
my stomach full of protests.
Lunchtime comes.
My fellow clerks escape,
full of dirty jokes and flirting.
I walk the shopper streets
weary, brooding and guilty,
burdened by fears of tomorrow.

Infection

Rebirthing old fears,
my body bodes an illness.
Is it disease, plague, bio-warfare?
My aching frame and head of tension
catapults me to dread ancient ills,
greedy thief yearning my life.
I sweat the office day away,
hungering the seclusion of my room,
where I will face old foes
more savage and pitiless
than my imagination.

Outdated

She always wears a grey, antique dress,
this holdout from another time,
bewildered in an antiseptic office
that sprouts incomprehensible machines
that replaced filing cabinets of comfort
where once she found refuge
from her fears of dismissal.

Retreat

At quitting time, in gathering mobs,
the frenzy flows, homeward bound.
In the crowded subways and buses,
demotic public transportation,
guides the drones to destinations
that may eradicate
the desolation of the office.

Bigots

How nice it must be
to laugh careless laughter
and talk, unconcerned with meanings.
In office prison
there are voices in adjoining rooms,
careless and irresponsible.
They sneer and snicker together,
but when they penetrate my isolation
all I hear is cars, cathouses, baseball,
and how something's gotta be done
about those anti-war demonstrations.
They babble back and forth
crammed with hate and drabness,
while each work day,
my hunger for friendship
desperates me a madness.

Overseer

There is a lady in a lake
somewhere, an affluence, a sleep,
a last forgetting without greed.
She rises from the shining water
as magical as ancient myths.
She cries:
"Oh my spirit slumbering brother,
"it's morning. Awake."
And I,
up till now unstirring,
turn restlessly at my desk,
as the glass and concrete voice
of the servant of Pharaoh
halts my escape
and sends my dream
crashing at my feet.

Simple Question

How sweet to walk at lunchtime
in brief escape from peon's curse.
I feel the sun creeping down my neck,
although I mostly snub that stranger,
coaxing me into forgetfulness.
Does everyone walk the lunchtime streets
hungering green fields and white beaches?
Should they drop their pencils
and pick up axes?

Infliction

My pens are children of hunger
bleeding words.
They sit in pleading rows
eager to be expended.
But I, the cruel torturer of silence,
do not write,
and make them suffer.

Deception

What is the value of time?
A young man sits at office desk
dreaming of writing, white beaches,
the softness of a woman
curled upon a midnight bed,
immersed in fantasies, yearnings.
He is possessed with guilt of daily failure,
the brief passing of joy,
memories of careless youth.
A slow, black panther stalks him,
claws unsheathed,
stops and listens to the evening whispers,
striking those who have no comfort,
then evaporates, a sudden mist,
lost to passions.

Hanging On

I am just a dreamer,
lost and dwindling.
Adrift in twentieth century madness,
I live the myth of city days,
but seek forgotten truths.
How easy I forget
the timeless hungers found in books.
How often I betray
my finer self, alone and proud,
lusting wisdom and compassion.
Exiled nine to five,
five stolen days each week,
I awaken each morning
rousing fears of joblessness and failure,
a dreary refugee, grey and crazed,
awaiting the weekend.

Indecision

This dullard
(is it really me?)
spending his office time
(alone, oppressed)
forced to listen daily
to demagogues of silly chatter
(betrayed, betrayed),
compelled to smile at bad jokes
(alas, Arjuna),
to ignore ugly mouths of prejudice
(Hamlet should have done it while he prayed.
Yup. When he prayed.),
while I wonder
could I do it at the water cooler?

Acceptance

Truly of the city now,
I, the sullen wanderer,
risk the subway crush,
the shoppers flow.
My mind is nine to five now
and my body is trapped by office walls,
but my soul waits with secret hope,
until I return to my poems.

Solitary Voyage

The grey song
of the morning subway
brings no joy
when we stand impaled
upon our neighbor's horns.
The implacable rush to work
in the morning of loss,
our unwilling time gone,
not even a trusted companion
on the foundering ship
of office daydreams.

Resignation

I am not bound by visions of power,
nor trapped by slim, white fingers of ambition,
bur weakened by the clamor of hunger
I often fail to do what must be done.

The days of waste, spent in office snare,
forced to do the work of dolts,
listening to their senseless chatter,
too aware of my own foolish words.

How to rise as nimble and light as smoke,
gracefully soaring high above the crowd,
becoming as pure and rare as cool, fresh air
filling my striving lungs with survival.

I know my aspirations are not dreams,
just desires waiting to be born,
but the long wait in bitterness and shame
blinds me to joy and binds me in sadness.

Indentured

This time of no daydreams,
another lost day at work.
The non-plowing sweat,
no pride in mindless labor.
So many hours wasted,
hours of never-regained time,
spent so quickly,
when all I wish
is to write my poems.

Distasteful Chore

Unwilling part of unsavory day,
when I, the singer of clerks,
the voice of monotony
thinks of a vision, softly,
to dream away the office hours.
I must lose the office snare
in the prison of my room . . . my mind . . . my life.
I only fare half well,
removing myself from my job,
but familiar with the perils of escape
I fear the return to work.

Escapist

Lost to dreams,
I, the nameless singer,
the rootless seeker,
spend my nine-to-five strength
a profligate reproduction
of carbon-copy clerks.

Diminishing Return

Another day that never seems to end
because I hobble, a drab Hephaestus,
absorbed in some moldy ago
that never allows joy
in morning appearance,
because I work
in a bore of days,
for paltry reward.
I would be a man of merit,
repelling the suit of maddened women,
clamorous, demanding
that this timid, office me
will become more than a mere clerk
and fulfill their fantasies.

Apprehension

I hate
the days of dreary torture
trapped in endless office waste
(I did not build a suitable career.
I dreamed of poetry.).

I loathe
my shallow, self-full soul,
swilled in righteousness and petty sneers
(I did not know the simple way
to love my brothers).

I fear
time's swifter passing,
the flying hours knell my workless nights
(I did not quell the lazy me
awaiting effortless grandeurs).

I hope
from this tedium and torment
a better me will grow
(knowing that weak endeavors
and shabby visions
may be my only glory).

Shelter

I a singer
in this unlove world,
fear in strange days,
running with the herd
in subway haste
where I dimly hope
the hip that presses mine
belongs to a woman.
That face of scowls
another impatient traveler
knocking down
old women, cripples, children,
any face that interferes
with speedy arrival,
my only escape
immersion in morning paper,
lurid as a running nose.

Repetition

O endless chain of Greek diners,
I find you near every job I take.
Can the same people be in each place?
They seem the same,
cursing the same job,
raving to a stranger
about the cheap lunch,
the same shifty eyes
prying curiously,
trying to see what I'm writing.

Drudgery

Tired and lost,
time passes with swift unkindness.
Buried by city millions,
my poems my only hope.
No more dreams for desolation,
each day so little change.
I go to work like others
in the morning of dreary consolation,
curse the moments until lunchtime,
eat a quick, tasteless meal,
flee to the sunshine of the park,
ringed by sad and hostile faces.
Then back to the office
for the remainder of the day,
slow, thwarting, maddening,
and finally go home,
worn from office spoliation
to brood about tomorrow.

Imagine

Whispering Majorca and Capri,
I magic myself,
capture three glyptodonts
in primordial elections,
sing a great poem of ultimate distance,
Betelgeuse, Aldebaran, Deneb,
some stranger than their remoteness.
I fall back to my desk
lover instantly erasing passion.
The longer dream has only two fingers.

On the Wheel

Another office day,
somehow more human.
Is it because of a woman
passioning me happy?
Is it from contentment,
a good night's writing?
I do not know,
but it is Friday
and the day does not pass fast enough.
Soon a weekend's freedom,
time to renew my strength
and hope to endure
another week at work.

Duplication

This large corporation of blankness,
built on the interchange
of meaningless figures,
how grey its members pass.
Long past sorrow and joy,
they find power in a Dictaphone
and somnambulistic and ear-plugged,
they never stop recording.

Tidal Surge

Security, that silly dream,
wooed in midnight fantasies,
my restless hunger seeking roots.
The pauper's fear,
my always unbelonging,
my atoms, insignificant,
finally begin to change.
In one week of passionate strangeness,
a new job,
published,
the hope of fulfillment.
Will this moment of recognition
defeat my ancient enemy,
my unsure self?

Lost Vision

Indelible desire,
planted deeper than a farmer's seed,
to create, instead of serf toil,
an escape from office exits.
I water you with words
that dilute action
and watch you slowly die.
I should do heroic labor
and fall as quenching rain,
instead I talk,
trapped in a cage of silence
and pace from wall to wall,
as the parched dream shrivels.

Pent

This time of no sleep
dreamless,
unrequiting all my workless fingers,
they sit
attached to idle arms
meant to strum lyres,
grasp spears,
stroke sloe-eyed maidens,
now idle, feckless
waiting for commitment
as they waste
in office confines.

Cyclic

So payday comes again
and I am opulent again,
until obligation, or extravagance,
sinks greedy fangs
into compensation
for two weeks labor.
Then poor again,
back to the daily fare,
hunger, insecurity, fantasy.

Confinement

I seem to be so alone,
each night trapped in my room,
each day spent at my job.
No friends, home, comfort,
just the daily vision . . .
daily failure.
Dare I name my hunger?
Just one hope, one satisfaction, writing.
Yet I neglect it.

Bitter Awakenings

We had a dream when we were young,
in the recess of a child's fun,
that of future glories sung,
merely waiting to be won.
First school, then work the pattern,
avoiding much pain and care,
then deceived by a slattern,
taking refuge in despair.
The pause that suffering brought,
the vision of elation
that brings all passions to naught,
lost in time's acceleration.

Transit

Subway faces
reduced from joy or care
to almost animal despair.
The fragments of laughter,
one brief and dear,
mirror to the constant fear.
When underground hordes emerge
they appear newborn
for a daring instant they return
to the shell of containment.

Inaction

How to drive away this anguish?
This bleak man haunting my days
with too unstealthy force,
capturing my power.
The fingers of desolation grip me relentlessly.
All day, all night, no rest;
ever battered in restless dreams.
The days pass with fleeting swiftness,
as I sit dreamless and inactive,
waiting for beginnings.

Breakout

Fires burn forever in the heart
loneliness breeds always in the mind,
fed with the barren fuel of repetitive days
we stampede to each weak diversion,
entwine ourselves within the coils of fantasy,
dream of legendary deeds—any escape
from the sterile confinement of the office.

Decay

While I am eroding at my job
the aging secretary glares at me
from her perch behind forever desk,
where she faithfully guards the time
of her oppressive employer.
She is another conspirator
to the assault on my senses
in this office degradation.

Loose Thread

I ponder the passing of time
as pompous as an ancient sage
trapped in paralytic sleep,
who knows the vision of waste.
The hours in the office unending,
the passionate hungers unsated,
the moments untempered by patience
bursting a myth on my frenzy,
while the somnolent spider of anger
toys with the thread of my future,
weaving no tomorrows.

Dozing

I ride the midnight train
intent on home
through night snow streets.
A flare-lovely woman
sits across the aisle.
We stare. I know
I will not talk to her
and she will not answer.
I want her. Her eyes read my hunger.
I know we shall not meet.
I shall not have her,
because the forest of my fumblings
confuses the freedom of mating,
so I sleep, wake, work,
consumed by visions
that confine me to my desk.

Regret

I sing of a woman
a stranger no longer,
known to my flesh,
touched by my feelings.
Our time so short
I fear she will not come again
and I weave a dark strand
from the tangle of her hair.
I awakened in the morning,
but she was not there.
Her yesterday smell, faint on the pillow,
hungered my remembrance.
When last we parted,
I, intent on office prison,
held her, not close enough.
Now I punish my neglect.

Harnessed

Beasts of burden
for exploiting bosses,
impatient of our arrival,
filled with urgency
more imminent than hate,
until our work is done,
coincidental with other workers,
whose only thought is home.

Futile Hopes

I am so tired of dreaming
and fearful of time's fleeting stay.
My words so weak they hardly say
the things that make my days a waste.
I am so sick of hoping
that each new day will bring release,
that all my foes will sue for peace,
my mind the battleground, my foe, desires.
Just to have each day alone
to write, unspent by job desolation,
to think, not bound by care's drab concentration,
this is what I struggle for.
Some friends, talk, laughter,
the fulfillment of people honest and sincere,
accepting me without pretense, talking without fear.
But most of all a woman
wiser and more beautiful than imagination.

Interrogation

The hesitant grope
for a few submissive words,
spawning dark escape
from many days spent
looking at each other,
brothers of nine-to-five soul,
and then we're submerged
in that unenthusiastic fumble:
Where did you go to school?
Who did you marry?
When did you die?
Or didn't you yet?

Yearnings

In my new clothes
I would strut the city,
a peacock poet,
but trapped in office greyness
my hunger fades
(because I only see the sky at lunchtime)
and visions of elegant women
completely disappear.

Reaffirm

This fruitless job
planned by some dim angel
surely bursting his halo
in joy at my despair.
Secure in his triumph,
he gloats on his comfortable cloud,
but then, shattered and desolate,
he watches me make again
a new effort at life.

Seasonal Touch

There is a magic quality of spring.
The hotter sun,
the softer wind,
the green dance of city trees.
People walk more slowly,
seduced by gentle weather.
Young girls in tight, short skirts
and bare midriffs
set young men dreaming.
And people sit in city parks
dawdling at lunchtime,
kinder, less bland.

Ignorance is . . .

I found a new job
and once again
am part of this frenetic world.
I rush, a mad citizen
aping my brothers.
I move through city masses
an indistinguishable swirl
of blind haste.
In the subway teeming,
on the streets of shoving,
in the shops of hurry,
I share the chaos
and the delusion
that life is stable.

Insurance

God bless the unemployment service
and its kind, courteous,
always helpful servants,
who make you wait two hours,
then send you elsewhere,
whose charitable favors
are yours for the begging,
who scrutinize your case
like misers guarding coffers,
and finally, with a regretful sigh,
approve your claim,
as if you're stealing from their children.
Yes, God bless the unemployment service,
and all its reluctant particles.

Park Moments

How nice to watch young women pass,
while sitting in the sunshine of a park.
Their high heels click
like hail assaulting corporate windows.
Their bright dresses light up my lunch hour.
The nearby traffic honks and roars.
People pass bewildered, sad,
barred from gladness
by impenetrable doors.
Yet somehow,
in the sunshine of the park,
I'm happy.

Niche

Altogether dreamless,
they serve their masters
with tired comprehension,
unquestioning as feudal serfs,
as they drift through office days
without access to advancement
by church or state.

Poems from *Songs of a Clerk* have appeared in:

Istanbul Literary Review, Agency Magazine, Fiction Press, Kyoto Journal, Poetry Life and Times, Rattlesnake Review, Written Word Literary Magazine, Pegasus Magazine, MadSwirl, YaSou!, Words Words Words, Juice Magazine, Struggle Magazine, Flutter Poetry Journal, Iddie, Strange Road, Halfway Down the Stair, Poetry Monthly, Poems Niederngasse, Leaf Pond, Red Fez, Pyramid Magaizne, Neveldetum, Mud Luscious, Pen Himilaya, Canopic Jar, Metromania Magazine, The Deliquent, AprilMayMarch 777, Third Reader, Swansea Poetry Magazine, Wanderings, Orbis, Poetry Monthly International, Full of Crow, Writer's Ink, New Mirage Quarterly, Calliope Nerve, Word Salad Poetry Magazine, Falling Star Magazine, The Legendary, 63 Channels, Vox Poetica, This Zine Will Change Your Life, Midwest Literary Magazine, Callused Hands, Work Literary Magazine, Mayo Review, Technicolor Magazine, Thunderdome, Record Magazine, Mud Job, The Ottawa Arts Review, Inwood Indiana, Gloom Cupboard, The Ofi Press. Indigo Mosaic published *Pavan and Other Poems*, that later became part of *Songs of a Clerk*.

About the Author

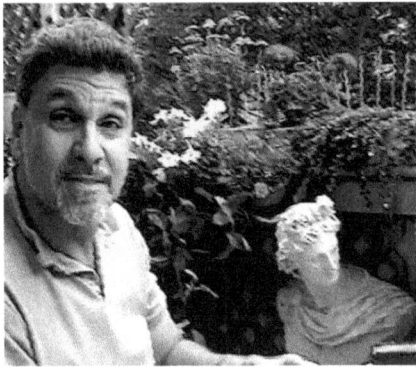

Gary Beck has spent most of his adult life as a theater director. He has had numerous published works including *Dawn in Cities, Extreme Change,* and the novel *Acts of Defiance.* Gary has also had numerous original plays and translations produced off Broadway, in New York City where he currently resides.